To Anthony

May the heart and soul always prosper

"History is the torch of the past
In the hands of the present
To light the way of the future"

Best Wishes

your mate

Conno

IN DARKNESS AND IN LIGHT

By

C. Enyo

Castalia Press

In Darkness and In Light

Published by
Castalia Press
In London, United Kingdom

www.castaliapress.com

First Edition published 2009

www.cenyo.co.uk

Dedicated to my parents
My family and friends

Always thankful to Our Father

God Bless

Contents

Section A

The Collection

Intro I

I find myself again drifting through clouds of smoke, walking desert plains of thought, getting caught and tangled in an emotional jungle that consumes us all. In mind I question every question that's been sung. Why do I exist? Is there meaning to our existence? Our map is designed by faith and institution, rules and restrictions, abuse and convictions; unarmed we battle constitution. There is sadly no solution to what can be humoured as human confusion, this utter failure to overcome desires and passion; our life a satire with a tiny ration of kindness. Betrayed by a kiss from ourselves, we sail, masked by a black veil. A life of blindness is a goose chase on endless trails. Though in this life we walk on for cause of justice, be it without clear sight; carrying on as soldiers, marching in darkness and in light.

PART 1

In Darkness

Intro II

Poetic justice is a knife that cuts through me in revelation. Tends to my longing for truth; quenches the thirst for knowledge, feeding starvation. Though an open cut can become infected and a virus is created that poisons your exposure and leads you astray. This plague grows stronger, creeping ever closer by the day. We pray but barely skim the surface as we bury our hearts deeper. Single ray lights this dim terrain, guarded by the Grim Reaper. Our markings washed away by rain, soul captive to the brain. In the valley of loss and the caverns of pain, we linger in shadows and in darkness remain.

Sorrow

Over crystal tears drop
Splatters of bitter thoughts
Crows fly in reverse
Following a slow hearse
Clocks tick in sorrow
Endless time they borrow
Without final destination
Heart tearing in retaliation
Mind ever growing brittle
Life a redefining riddle

Night calls thieving hour
Trespassers stealing power
Belief slowly shatters
Dreams cease to matter
Betrayal lingers leeching
Proud wounds bleeding
Symbols irritate torment
Spirit buried in cement
The growing seed of sorrow
Will feed again tomorrow

Dawning Cold

Pain consumed has become identity
Name assumed as some fraternity
Situation a patent to the rejected
Nation descent from being protected

Alone she swims rivers of sorrow
Forgone is her home of tomorrow
By mass minority her tag copy-written
Spirit a rag as this dark horse is ridden

Haunting nights bring restless calm
Daunting fights in daylight harm
Needles and pipes the Christmas décor
Morning unravels more gifts that sore

White coated dust with a dawning cold
This hated lust has the morning foretold
Bated trust leaves harvest of rotten corn
Flowers drop upon marked stone to mourn

The Small Giant

Platinum ribbons dance
Upon silky soft quilts
Scattered diamonds glitter
A giant passes high on stilts

Off came his hat, Hello Crow
Black bird gave a blank stare
What news my good fellow
Carries fresh the morning air

Now beware good man
For there will be frost
Watch for the wonderers
Claiming to be lost

Time sought with no map
Wounded snake slithered
He leaned down to pick it up
Passing owl whispered
It might be a trap

Though the little life suffers
And I am big and strong
To ignore doesn't truly matter
The wise owl could be wrong

The snake hissed a smile

It slithered down his waist
Wrapped around his stilts
And snuck a little taste

The giant cried painfully
Tilting towards the ground
Snake laughed shamefully
A scary, eerie sound

Nowhere to be found
Motionless the giant now lay
The snake looked around
Then slithered away

Platinum ribbons embrace
Fresh sky born tears
The sleeping small giant
Left to the mercy of his peers

Deluded Promises

Serene voices whisper for comfort
Amongst savage screams of treason
They try to reason with your pain
In vain gamblers of faith pretend
As masses wait to raise the dead

Through material desert planes
Zombies walk along side the living
Giving hints of their existence
The resistance blind with ambition
Young rebels with no true mission

Rain will come to wash the land
And cool this concrete heat
Light so bright, sight is revoked
Morals eluded in mirror swords
Deluded promises of fiscal lords

Guitar stringing silent chords

Idealism

Spawned in liberation
Strengthened by laughter
Weakened in sadness

Tickled with suggestion
Tormented by temptation
Satisfied with relief

Trialled by tribulations
Enslaved by possessions
Liberated by revelations

Undressed by the artist
Raped by the poet
Murdered by the writer

Lost in society
Revoked by authority
Buried in bureaucracy

Reach the Sun

Beneath lustful skies
Upon virgin lands
Our gestures aiding lies
Poisoned by our hands
The innocent waters run
Stuck in sinking sand
We reach to catch the sun
And slowly die inside

Haunted Mansion

Endless days, sleepless nights
Hunting to find one thats right
Bait is wrong, line won't bite
Seeking love without clear sight

In misery alone with desperation
Ignorant to her real temptation
Aphrodite, a hotlist compilation
Ignorant truth, a mere revelation

Not seeking their Queen to be
Nor a game to fulfil misery
"Just to satisfy the animal in me"
To satisfy a spirit that is but free

Merely to find that mind alike
Not a matter of black or white
Or body that is loose or tight
Maturity sought to come to light

Wet the lips with liquid passion
Silky skin touch, a sexual ration
Tongue upon, delivers sanction
Body now a haunted mansion

Submission

Through chain and shackle, tears streamline
Along rope over hardened breast, cheek and thigh
Restricted by vine of passion, submission is born
Sensation sharpened of a body wrapped with thorn
Her pain, in her smile shapes a skin-lit shine
Lip and nipple hard swollen, splashed with red wine
Stimulating screams accompany strikes upon her pose
Wet flesh shaded pink, like with dew a morning rose
In disciplined devotion with pain herself she finds
Though the pain she searches, is the pain of mine

Fatal Passion

Sensual passion in the touch of a petal
Pain experienced subsides and settles
Rose discovered among thorn and nettle
Beauty alluring, penetrating and fatal

PART 2

In Light

Intro III

Hope is a matter of heart. Conviction is a matter of mind. At the end of every rainbow is a treasure for the kind. I find that to love is easy, when the heart is free. Every tree, flower and creature, offers fractions of the key; unlock your soul and relieve yourself of this material toll. Piece together the puzzle and unravel this knot. It is a shame to detain discovering the worthlessness you have got and the treasures you have not; or those you have lost. Time will only be a friend if you chose it to be; otherwise it can be a devious enemy. Judge not those of faith because they seek relief in common belief; humility needs great potency of moral strength. Do not fear the Dark, even when life is dim. A true seeker will always find light from within.

Chariots of Fire

Three chariots of fire
Crash upon possessed seas
Shadows dance in flames
In shame, desire flees

Darkness again descends
Vengeance cast now worse
Blanketing miles over man
From sand returns this curse

Lashes induce shivers
In favour of forgone fight
Thorns crown thy brother
Father, giver of light

Be it in blood written
Message eternally engraved
Future decoded by past
Fast we ridden and betrayed

Whence knights tackle
Weak are those bold and brave
Abandoning their only armour
Farmer in shackles, enslaved

Tears cleanse the lands

War continues to plague
Broken wings of fallen angels
Lost souls brand old trade

Those chariots deserted
Dismay alone remains
No stars for navigation
Damnation reverts to shame

From the veins we drink
And of body our hunger fed
An ugly thirst to quench
In stench we sink the dead

Ignore the poor and needy
Disregard the starved to die
In blindness discover a sham
Man, a seedy, greedy lie

Upon these Chariots of fire
Hope is still conveyed
Valley low to mountain high
Dark skies retire and fade

Winter Rose

The winter had an early spawn
From among remains of snow
A rose begun to grow by dawn
Reason of phenomena unknown

In blizzards and thrashing rain
Sweeping winds and icy hail
Strong it stood to withhold pain
To grow this rose would not fail

Beneath a single ray of light
Dressed in morning vapour dew
The little life continued to fight
Blooming as a rarity among few

In the cold and gloomy mist
A man walked upon crisp ground
Stepping beside with a near miss
The blossom this stranger found

His garden the winter had froze
Leaving roughened fingers numb
Now once again with this rose
He could create what he had begun

This rose a mystical anomaly
Of natures sweet secrets untold

It had its own fine harmony
And needed little light to grow

Through seasons the years past
It proliferated dozens more
Though life is not created to last
This rose exempt to nature's law

A simple metaphor holds a clue
To the product of earths love
The beauty behind it simply true
Like the loyalty of a paired dove

Roses are wonderful and many
Though in this singular he knew
He found the lucky bronze penny
And forever his rare rose is you

Halkidiki

The calm waves wash away remains of yesterday.
Stars constellate a formation of love,
As passion falls in the amber leaves of days to come.
It is in the spring droplets of rain and the vapour dew of May
That people will discover laughter and pain.
A ladybird will sip on life from the petal that settles in the wind.
Faith is found by a farmer in the fresh ocean breeze
And the fisherman discovers his lover, in the evergreen of old olive trees.
On their knees, the mountains praise the heavens, tickled by the soothing sea.
The worker's day, finds closure in a cup of wildly brewed tea.
Marble has crumbled and thyme spread amidst lavender.
Gods find time in an open-ended calendar, to retire with an evening fire,
As night dawns on Halkidiki; Greece now sleeps peacefully.

Final Test

When I leave life
Shed no tears
It's a sharp knife
Cutting deep
To carry fears

I sing this note
Hold no regrets
It's a sinking boat
To a watery grave
On a long stretch

Finally lay to rest
I close my eyes
The final test
To face truth
I now realise

What I loved
And left behind
What I hated
And kept alive
Inside my mind

Walk On

Go on my son
Run
Deep into dark
Seek those caverns
Go far
Follow the rain
Cleanse pain
Ask the unimaginable
Go insane

Laugh cry breath
Doubt seek believe

Pledge no allegiance
March with the dead
No law of obedience
Live free instead
Bask in sensations
Feed desire
Satisfy all temptations
Before you retire

Empty handed return
Many years from now
Soul branded by burns
Before eternity bow

Plead mercy to a mirror
Taste every bitter thought

Reach around body
Blood metal wood
Mind full of worries
I am sorry, is a lie
Did all you could
Yet we live to die

Kiss symbol
Replenish strength
Run
Chase after death

Go on my son
Walk without fear
You're never gonna die
Over hilltops fly
On a tear
Float through sky

And If your travels
Ever lead you home
Go on my son
Walk on

Apocalypse

The ground will rumble in crumbling pain
The skies will crack with blistering anger
A drought is to come,
High waves will drown the living
Upon which stealing fires ride,
Lighting up the devil's night, scolding pray
Reducing to ashes the cometh of a new day

Kingdom rise as kingdom come
Night will set with this adherence of rule,
Good men treated as mules
Mothers and daughters subjected to the cruel,
Wicked will be the choice of living
Many will fail to last,
Losses of this war
Spent on reliance
Missing in defiance

The sun will find its way many years later
The burnt earth will be painted gold,
The court of justice will open in session
The years will be weighed in affliction
Sentencing eternal conviction,
Men's hearts returned to their chests
The land now ready to recover,
Sprouts its first hope,
In a little white flower

In Darkness and In Light

Ground upon which you walk
Now open like a crooked door
Automated movement
Your mechanical transmission
Spirit a neglected item
Dusty on the shelf of a store
A contradiction defines it all
You petition for that much more
Crippling emotion
Eroding notion
This is the score
Devotion to your dark lord

Let in new light
To freshen gloom
Some fight the doom
And some die too soon
A little robin sings on the outside
From within the grasp of a hawk
Mothered by the beast
Freed from the hunter
Reversing the norm
I am born again
Tasting new life
From within the rage of this storm

Take my brother
Rape our bodies torn
In Dark I linger on
But there is a call
Destination for the new age boy
Broken toy, remains on the shelf
There is no one else
For man reaches not a hand out
This is the offering of heart
Worldly morals abandon any right
Step now into sight
Remember there is still hope
For we live in darkness and in light

Conclusion

Day slips away and night creeps in. The red coal now glows a gentle green. We are cursed with desires and freed with disease. I know you will shed dry tears over all these, fears; as I have also done. Clear your thinking of this captive drinking and sober the spirit. Maybe then you will feel it; this simplicity of truth that we all ignore. Do not grieve for your loss, for the dead and for the mould you taste in your daily bread. Instead be thankful for this grace; bad timing and this dreadful place. Humour yourself and measure the fullness of your empty glass. All that is bad will pass, with our time of rebirth; our home is not here on Earth. Do not pity the crippled or sick. Their wings may spread further than you think. Be concerned for those who seem perfect or superior. Deem this not as the right criteria; their hearts might be inferior. I have now come to my conclusion. What we desire and need is an illusion. We are raised in material confusion and this is why we live in Darkness. Nonetheless, the world is full of loveliness. I now know, I must be simple in my ways and grow humble in my heart. It is not easy to achieve but to try, is a start. Then, on we must fight, so that we can live in Light.

Section B

Five **PIECES** of **ESSENCE**

PIECE 1 - Kingdom of Man

Born in a lustful pit of despair, we grow, unaware.
Endless branches of the apple tree, tap upon a venomous attraction, offering a taste of satisfaction, to feed desire.
Substances take us higher, seeking an ultimatum of escape.
We forgo logic of heart for that of mind.
We think of feelings instead of feeling thoughts.
I have entered in a crawl, on hands and knees through disease and tasted all; hands in muck, screaming fuck, from the centre of my battlefield, shielding my brother, betraying mother and father, and murdering my other, half; whilst I assassinate my mirror reflection, for an empty laugh.
Yesterday's son was wired, today's wireless.
Tomorrow's daughters drop tears of emptiness.
Increasingly man fails this test, ever more withdrawn from reality; sharper minds of shallower souls consumed by vanity.
Life is but a short journey leading to one particular day, a singular moment within this insanity.
Many pray and many more words are lost every day in empty spaces; vacuums of enslaved races, lost lives and frightened faces, with no ears to truly hear the future's call.
This kingdom shall fall and with it, will sink all.

PIECE 2 - Kingdom of Heart

Passion of body, wrapped in thorn, penetrates this organ of blood; of love.

We are born in soft satin quilts and sink deep within these sheets, in favour of flesh.

Upbringing, routed through image and sound, nailing us down against lucid ground; misplaced we seek ourselves in the lost and found.

Uncover this naked body and open old wounds with roughened hands.

I am bleeding truth and scarring with lies.

From the skies came light and from the earth's core, our demise.

From the epicentre great fires exuberate, melting our touch.

Hot lava streams within our veins; children of pain.

In the desert I seek comfort of rain, to wash away this eternal stain but I remain, dirty.

We roll in the mud of ecstasy, harmony of touch and kiss; tyranny of physical bliss; missing the true point and slipping further into dark.

That spark of heart, revives infatuation of mind, sensation of an unreal kind; a non existent love.

Try to look deeper and you will discover, in the rubble of collapsed moral and deluded emotion; a mortal feeling for your brother, within your secluded corrosion.

Protect thy kingdom from this burning lust, returning to thy people peace.

Let the old future be new past and allow for the dawning of an era of good souls.

Aphrodite will not be the bearer of warmth but of cold.

Cupid has grown old and Hermes is but a haunting, daunting man.

Rid him from your heart and start again, to build a dam, over this exposed sham.

The secret to meditation lies in the appreciation for the rhythm of your heart beat.

For this kingdom can only be ruled by one and not by the collective of many; men or fleet.

PIECE 3 - Flesh and Blood

Life given through physical lock will bring ticking to your clock, as this race sets in motion.
Your innocent lotion quickly rinsed, life chord ripped and now you walk alone; wonderer with no home.
Forgone is your purity, in an obscurity of mankind.
Only in search can you ever find truth and sanity of mind.
Behold those who adore you and those who hate and ignore you.
Turn your back on offering of excitement and revelation, for only in love can there be improvement and delegation; of liberation.
Be kind to parents and the elderly for we are products of their maternity; servants of their infidelity, as we give the future an uncertainty and become the serpents.
Disturbance is the betrayal of their love, disrespecting their fight to survive; a war so that we may have life.
We cut loose with this shameful knife and strife for excellence; a conditional purulence; misinterpreted diagnosis, of our gnosis.
Chose wisely your immediate circle, those friends and lend a hand to those in need.
Think not of your greed but feed the living in despair; it is divine to care.
Be not cynical; a helping hand of a stranger is nothing short of a miracle.
The love of friends and neighbours is not heritable.

Though it may be pleasurable and it can be charitable, this love is measurable, by a short string; it can prove unsustainable and often heretical, in the truth it will bring.
Do not take for granted flesh and blood.
For whether linked by gene or by none; we are all buried as one.

PIECE 4 - Life and Death

I sit upon old roof tops that have been devoured by a human hunger for concrete and iron.

The mountains are now partial, hidden in the mists of construction.

Open space is not a natural familiarity to my generation, unlike the elements of isolation and despair.

Natural green seems pretty to my eyes but I struggle to understand why.

Is grey not the natural colour of the sky?

I ask myself, since the mind is pleased why does the heart cry?

Is it not the norm to concern our selves with beauty, or to cheat and lie?

Is there any value to the world I have been offered, once I die?

So tell me friend, neighbour, parent, Grandparent, priest, lover, dearest Godfather; what is the point to my existence?

Is it to taste every fruit from every tree; to see all there is to see and be the best I can be?

If so, how can the blind live happy and how can one incarcerated, be free?

My father said, son, if anything, salvage everything, in every memory; only this will be kept in eternity.

My priest said son, a real man, is one strong enough to be humble and repent.

My mother says, son, never forget, to be kind, sincere and decent.

These are the three secrets, I am told, to gracefully growing old.

But my friend, lover, child, son or daughter, the world is wild and it is hard to progress righteously, as we scold ourselves and others mindlessly; slaughtering ethics, as faithless heretics.

The knowledge and accomplishment I now have to pass on, is only a drop in a vast ocean.

First we are born; live a short while and then we are gone.

We act as if this cycle is an endless loop; though it is not long.

The chance to prosper for the soul is forgone, in every moment; remember you don't own it!

I arrived in the cold early hours of December, so we celebrate to remember.

Unknown is the day I will leave and yet that is the day I shall be set free; so celebrate this victory, in my memory.

My greatest achievement will be if this day is one of clarity; leaving behind love and harmony.

I am tired of social sanity and seek a way out of the labyrinth.

I give my broken compass to the guidance of divine hands as I walk away from man and sit on the metaphor of clouds; proud I float in prayer, holding firmly upon my maker.

Material captivity is a war zone in which we battle for salvation; for freedom a test.

This, my child, is life and death.

PIECE 5 - Heaven and Hell

Every step leads to a path, every path, to a crossroad.
Every crossroad brings choice, every choice calls for a
decision.
A decision will dictate direction and every direction, heads to
a checkpoint.
Your every checkpoint is a milestone, of right and wrong,
time cometh and time gone.
There is condition to every way of life, state of mind and that
of soul.
Angels fall and daemons rise.
Men die and spirits live on.
Time brings the war closer to the forefront.
Cursed whore clenches her baby tight, close to her chest.
Rich men who pass spit at her in disrespect.
Warriors are hung from trees by their neck.
Profits are lost for words.
This world, so small, can be placed in a locket, worn by a little
girl who is unaware.
They stare, as she grows to be the prostitute that will dare to
repent.
Her tears reflect the haunting laughter of those who judge
her shame, though they are members of the brotherhood to
blame; souls tagged by a single name.
The homeless drunk, cried from the pain, before his final
night.
A neighbourhood priest prays to fight; he has seen the inner
being, pleading for peace.

I once ceased, to believe.

I now see, though distorted by the mask I wore, I am perhaps now, only partially free.

The mirror, like scissors, cut and tore this cloth by which I have been embalmed.

I have become unarmed.

Bare, I am kept from harm by a single symbol that hangs from the base of my head; I can now feel the dead, for they are the living; they breathe inside of us, inside of me.

And it is they who are grieving, for us, for humanity; those who still exist as matter and dust, abiding by the laws of flaws and lust.

The home of God and that of the Devil can not be geographically located; they exist within our confinements, both the physical and that not.

Both Lords live within our own; our body their thrown; our soul their kingdom.

We are the means for this energy to grow, this Darkness or Light; it is solely our individual fight and no other person's, creature's or being's.

And despite this, we ignore our reality and press deep into vanity; happily consuming the poison of material pleasure, savouring not the fasting that will measure the right to the only one true treasure.

Is patience not a virtue?

This I think, we all know to be so; yet we laugh at those who show, this attribute; this ability to grow.

So it will be in the choices you take and the paths you walk that will lead you to your destination; have no hesitation.

Here you will find your true home; soldier of Rome.

If you choose to sleigh your brother, scold your sister and sell, your moral ground; Hell is where you will be found.

If you fight for what is right, repent and lent your offering to your fellow man; Heaven is where you will stand.

It is in this life that you will grow with either condition; this is your only true mission.

Your final chance will rest in the crossing to the other side; have no pride.

It is easy to preach and say, or even to 'know' what is right. I have heard these words I now share with you, countless times; I've written them in lyrics and rhymes.

Whether they are false or true, to abide by them is the Everest of tasks, both for me and for you.

But if you look deep within your inner side, do you not identify; hear that cry, for help?

As we live in the depth of a deep dark, damp narrow well; is this not Hell?

And when we achieve to break those barriers that restrict our love, offer instead of take, make instead of break and escape those seven sins; is this not Heaven that we are in?

If we simply tried and escaped our own lies, within us we can all truly tell; which Heaven is and which Hell.